Lyrics and Poetry

from late in the 20TH Century

by

MARTIN FAWKES

---

oceandeep
PRESS

All works © Martin Fawkes

Modern World © 1985

If The Words Get In The Way, I've Seen It, Ladder, Longing, Pictures, Tender Human Heart © 1987

Bonfire, Coat, Goodbye, A New Town, Tide, What © 1989

Engraved In Light, Guilty By Word Association, 99, Stand Your Ground, Walk Away From The Fire, Walk In The Water © 1990

All That Love Is, Hollowed Out, I Love You, Land Ho, Nice Talk (Conversation For Beginners) © 1991

King's Vengeance, Speak Louder © 1993

A Sense Of It, Birds, Cut, Grace, Long Gone, Long To Come, Over, Recover Me, Safe, Seventy Seven Seconds, Shake Down, South, Told, Wine and Water, Why Can't I Hold You? © 1995

B'Boom, Butterfly, Faux Pas, Gardensong, Hear, House, Prodigalus (Don't Think You Can't Come Back), Smith, The Hour We Knew Nothing of Each Other, Write © 1996

Blood, Map, Nobody Knows, Seldom Random, Wordstuff, You Will Go Free © 1997

Far From Home, More Seconds, Never, Old Friends, Right On Time, Where © 1998

Rain © 2011 Worth © 2012

Cover image and interior artwork adapted from "St. Albans Starlight" by Chris Fawkes © www.chrisfawkes.com

TO CUT
 A LONG STORY
 SHORT

ISBN 978-0-6456419-3-6

Published by
OCEANDEEP
PO Box 4264
Geelong VIC 3220 Australia
www.oceandeep.au

I can see my glass is half full,
> but of course, I did order a double.
>> Fran Lebowitz

Poetry and Lyrics
from late in the 20TH Century
by
MARTIN FAWKES

---

oceandeep
PRESS

CONTENTS

PART ONE: ONCE UPON A TIME

99 ❋ A Sense Of It ❋ All That Love Is ❋ B'Boom ❋ Birds ❋ Blood ❋ Bonfire ❋ Butterfly ❋ Coat ❋ Cut ❋ Engraved In Light ❋ Far From Home ❋ Faux Pas ❋ Gardensong ❋ Goodbye ❋ Grace

PART TWO: IN THE DEEP DARK WOODS

Guilty By Word Association ❋ Hear ❋ Hollowed Out ❋ The Hour We Knew Nothing of Each Other ❋ House ❋ I Love You ❋ If The Words Get In The Way ❋ I've Seen It ❋ King's Vengeance ❋ Ladder ❋ Land Ho ❋ Long Gone, Long To Come ❋ Longing ❋ Map ❋ Modern World

PART THREE: IN A LITTLE HOUSE THERE LIVED

More Seconds ❋ Never ❋ A New Town ❋ Nice Talk (Conversation For Beginners) ❋ Nobody Knows ❋ Old Friends ❋ Over ❋ Pictures ❋ Prodigalus (Don't Think You Can't Come Back) ❋ Rain ❋ Recover Me ❋ Right On Time ❋ Safe ❋ Seldom Random ❋ Seventy Seven Seconds ❋ Shake Down

PART FOUR: AND HAPPILY EVER AFTER

Smith ❋ South ❋ Speak Louder ❋ Stand Your Ground ❋ Tender Human Heart ❋ Tide ❋ Told ❋ Walk Away From The Fire ❋ Walk In The Water ❋ What ❋ Where ❋ Why Can't I Hold You? ❋ Wine and Water ❋ Wordstuff ❋ Worth ❋ Write ❋ You Will Go Free

AN INTRODUCTION:

There's an old saying, I think you know it: "Talk is cheap".

But maybe there's more to it than that. Maybe it should, or could, really read; "talk is cheap, but conversation is priceless".

One of the joyous things in my life has been growing up with several siblings, a brother and three sisters, plus parents, in-laws, offspring, relatives and all the joys of a talkative, talkative family. Ask us anything, anything at all, and sometimes you'll get a direct answer.

Oh, but how much more fun to tell you that answer, eventually, along with all the steps, stumbles and overcomings it took to get there?

Yeah. Yeah, yeah. Got a minute?

Which brings us to this. A brand new edition of my second poetry & lyric collection, first released prior to the turn of the Century. Speaking of things beyond words, sometimes so much to say I have to use less words to get it all across.

To Cut a Long Story Short: it's all there, all of it, but between the lines, and in them.

Enjoy!

once upon a time

99

The door was always open
But you never did come in
Although I lit the welcome fires
And everything

I had waited for so long
To hear that knock upon my door
But now my bags are packed
It's you I'm looking for

Though there be ninety-nine at home
Still I'd come to find you
Although ninety-nine at home
Still I'd seek to see
Your wounded heart
And end its wandering
And bring your lonely heart
Back home to me

I'd climb the highest mountain
To bring you shelter from the storm
Though it cost me everything
To keep you warm
And if you're hurt and bleeding
If you're cold and bruised and tired
If all you have is soaked in rain and mire
Let your heart cry out for freedom
Let your spirit cry release
Because I'm searching
I will come to set you free

Though there be ninety-nine at home
Still I'd come to find you
Although ninety-nine at home
Still I'd seek to see
Your wounded heart
And end its wandering
And bring your lonely heart
Back home to me

A SENSE OF IT

Once I read a story
Not knowing where to look
Such sense becomes a bouquet
Of ends and beginnings

Then I knew some stories
And recognized the tale
More ends and ends
Some beginnings

Such sense becomes a bouquet
Such a sense of it
Such a sense of it
Where will it end?
Where will it all begin?

Once I became a story
In someone else's book
Let it be more than words
More than talk
More than just a quiet read in the corner

Sensible like a bouquet
Of ends
And beginnings
And all the lovely
In betweens

ALL THAT LOVE IS

I'll tie my hand to your hand
Before we start down this road
And though the journey be long
I will stay by your side
Wherever you go

Gentle and kind
Humble and true
I want to be
All that love is
For you

I'll bind my heart to your heart
As we start this new page
Let our lives tell the story
Of a love once begun
Lasting age unto age

Gentle and kind
Humble and true
I want to be
All that love is
For you

I will lay down my life
As a sacrifice of love

B'BOOM

Cannon thunder standing shaker
Portents of unsettling drifting loosened moorings
Battens open hatches break down in that moment
Couldn't stop the disassociations
Couldn't stop the disassociations

BIRDS

There are birds we dare not name
Flying
Across our mutual landscape
Birds that bring us the twigs
And feathers
Whose call we learn to sing together
Flying
Flying nameless
One day we will name them
But not yet

BLOOD

bloodshedformebloodshedformeonceiwasblindbutno
wiseeicanseewashedintheliquidturnedsindarktosnow
wouldneverhaveknowntellmehowcouldihaveknownb
utsomebodytoldmesosimpleasonetwoandsoonetceter
aoncethingsweresepticbutnowsocleansocleanicouldn
otwashawaywhatadebticouldneverrepaythankgodforr
ippingupthebutchersbillsonlyonesacrificenecessaryonc
eandforevertodoawaywiththebloodshedlastofallhisow
nbloodwassheditwashedawaymySIN

BONFIRE

Set a match to my deeds of straw
Set aflame
And burn my fingers
Till I touch them no more
Consume in fire the creeping death
That lets me speak then rest
And loses touch
With incorruptible stuff

Mine own self become hollow man
If ever true then let me be again
My crown is done, 'tis broke in two
Cast into heat and fuse to one anew

BUTTERFLY

One foot in front of another
Led you to this town
And now your uncertain heart
Is saying turn around
But do not feel you have a thing to prove
To find yourself known and valued
A house and yard, husband and kid
Belonging to another wife
It's not your worry
Not your life to live like that
Poor butterfly
Be free
Trust your gossamer wings
Your fragile gossamer wings
Be free

COAT

Coat
Heavy coat
On my shoulders
Long
Coat
Long coat
Down my back
Long heavy coat

Like guilt
Long heavy guilt
On my shoulders
Down my back
Long heavy guilt

I want
To take
My coat off
But I like the cloth
From which it is made

CUT

To cut and spill the earth
Penetrated by the plough
So what is working worth
If all is failing now
Before this all began
A garden of desire
The soil and seed of man
Descends to funeral pyre

ENGRAVED IN LIGHT

You write a story on a sensitive page
Engrave an image, catch a moment in colour
You hold a thought for another age
Click and there's a heartbeat
Click and there's another

You breathe a misty breath on glassy panes
Ignite a dream land, new worlds to discover
You seek the forest where the mystery wanes
Opened in a heartbeat
Beating with an Other

And all will be revealed
That has been concealed
All will be revealed
That has been concealed

Hold to the fingerprints of other days
Ageless mystery, providing your cover
A touch of holy oil will change your ways
Listen for the heartbeat
Listen for the other

And all will be revealed
That has been concealed
All will be revealed
That has been concealed

FAR FROM HOME

Far from home
I feel like I'm so far from home
I've put matches to the bridges
Locked up old homes and thrown away the key
All that's left here is just my baggage and me
My baggage and me

So far from home
I've been travelling so far from home
Not like I had much choice
I had to come once I'd heard your voice
Didn't know if you were calling out to me
It sounded like my name
So, somehow, I came

Away from home
I went for a walk
And found myself so far from where I began
Sometimes I stumbled and crawled
And sighed and looked the other way
But still I was listening

Sometimes it feels like I'm on a journey in a foreign land
It's only the landmarks look the same
The inner geography, it's like nowhere I have been
But now, somehow, I'm here
So let's begin

FAUX PAS

My back is knotted
With the cords of treacherous truths
Innocently opened out without warning
When silence would have seemed discreet
Don't want to say that yet
Not now
Not here
Quiet! Please!
Oh no, how do I acknowledge
Clear up
Clarify
Without exposing nerves and veins
Don't want to be vulnerable
Don't want to be so misunderstood
Don't want in the open
What is half done in the not open
Leave off, stop!
Too late, spoken
Open
But not open
Clearly unclear
Merde

GARDENSONG

Drawn down thunder
Such an innocent little lie
Drawing down such thunder from the sky

Goodbye blue bliss
Seal it with a forlorn kiss
Skins and hidden shame
Farewell to thunder

Serpent legs for dinner
Let him crawl (don't need those limbs no more)
Defiant goes down to dust
We dare not laugh
Bit the lie
And now we die

Drawn down thunder
Such an innocent little lie
Drawing down such thunder from the sky

Goodbye blue bliss
Seal it with a forlorn kiss
Skins and hidden shame
Farewell to thunder
Farewell to thunder

GOODBYE

You take the path of least resistance
You're leaving with the tide
You'll soon be washed
Out of existence
Is this goodbye?

You never stand for what you stood for
No lasting passion in your eyes
The flames die down to ashen smouldering
Is this goodbye?

Open up at His insistence
Spirit burn with holy fire
Fight to the shore of true existence
And not goodbye

GRACE

Grace bought me a new shirt
Such long sleeves
Oh look at me!
Ah! Look at Grace who paid for this
Thank you Grace

Mercy bought me a new life
A new kind of life

Ransom bought me a new freedom

Jesus is building me a new house

in the deep,
dark woods

GUILTY BY WORD ASSOCIATION

Cork	chalk
blackboard	blackbird
birdhouse	cage
green parrot	cockatoo
two for the price of one	one Lord one faith one baptism
swim underwater	die
go to heaven	heaven is a wonderful place
placemat	dinner
word of God is milk and meat	meet me here
hear and obey	trust and obey
baptism	man with glasses stands in the water
water and fire	burn
chaff	horses on the wind
apocalypse	fire and thunder
judgement	wrath
doom (for some)	Satan cast into the pit
Mercy on me o God!	
let me count in the	let me count in the
now before You come again.	now before You come again.

HEAR

I can't hear you
From here
Maybe I'll move a little closer
Can't expect you to call out louder
Couldn't wait for mind readings
Resurrections, respirations
Incarnations pre and post and re
I'm sort of straining I can't hear
You can you hear me?

HOLLOWED OUT

Once upon a time I was a plank of wood
Until the carpenter came
Now I'm a boat to sail the seas
Now I'm a cup from which to drink
A candlestick holder
A cane, a walking stick
Now I've been carved, cut
Hollowed out

Once upon a time I was a plank of wood
Until the carpenter came
With saw and knife and tools
To measure my potential
To cut away the not useful
To reveal a work of art held captive

Hammer striking chisel
Barking wood
Chips splinter spray and fall
Scraping, sawing, cutting, gouging. carving
These instruments rip and tear my turgid flesh
Until I stand
A boat, a cup
A candlestick holder
I've been carved, cut
Hollowed out

THE HOUR WE KNEW NOTHING
OF EACH OTHER

Walking down leaf littered back streets
Heading home, so far home
Train ride upon train ride from here
All I've seen is next to nothing
How could I know what you needed to know?
Thinking thoughts
Brief thoughts (but frequent)
About the brief trusting moments
When I looked into your eyes
And spoke
Not knowing your not knowing
Only saying what I was saying

And the clock ticks towards another hour
I'd heard you on the radio
Then you were sitting there
I'd been asked to tell you all I could
I looked into your trusting eyes
I spoke
But did not know
What you needed to know
Until now

HOUSE

Every house in the
World needs a doormat
For its front door

Someone to lay down
Their life
And clean
The muddy feet
Of the ignorant

I LOVE YOU

I lied so you wouldn't be alone
But deep down I guess I knew
That this would bring it all undone
Like some protected treasure
I'd kept these thoughts from view
Then let the words be spoken
Before their time was due

Once uttered then regretted
Made a corpse where life once played
Hollow thud of words not meant
Some comfort, like a chilling thought
I'm sorry for the doubts I wrought

I'VE SEEN IT

Say you dream of freedom, I've seen it
You say you long for liberty
A light inside to shine for thee
Reduce your chains to chalk
And break them easily

I've seen it in a life
I've seen it in a death
I've seen a dead man live and breathe
An everlasting breath
I've seen it in the truth
Of resurrected lives
I've seen it in the book
I want to see it in your eyes

Say you dream a future, I've seen one
You look for hope in foolish things
As scarecrows masquerade as kings
But worlds compared to heaven
Won't mean anything

I've seen it in a life
I've seen it in a death
I've seen a dead man live and breathe
An everlasting breath
I've seen it in the truth
Of resurrected lives
I've seen it in the book
I want to see it in your eyes

I've seen it
I want to see it

IF THE WORDS GET IN THE WAY

If I tried to say it would you listen
If I tried to speak it would you listen
Would you hear a thing I say

If I wrote it for you would you read it
What would it take to show how much you need it
Would you hear a thing I say

If the words get in the way
I pray that you will see
If the words get in the way
Spirit set you free

If I tried to say it could you hear it
Would you hear another way than I mean it
Would you hear a thing I say

If the words get in the way
I pray that you will see
If the words get in the way
Spirit set you free

Sometimes I think my hopes
Are worth their wait in tears
Sometimes I wonder if you'll see
I pray the hand of God
Will wipe away your tears
And help you see and hear it
And help you hear and see

KING'S VENGEANCE

You made me swallow a bitter pill
When all I wanted was a home cooked meal
But one day, one day I know...

You wore a velvet glove on iron hand
Tried to destroy the boy inside the man
But one day, one day I know...

The King's vengeance will come
The King's vengeance will come
It's not mine to repay
I'm just waiting for the day
When the King's vengeance will come

So tell me would you bite the hand that feeds
Could you sever that which brings you to your knees
Well one day, one day I know...

The King's vengeance will come
The King's vengeance will come
It's not mine to repay
I'm just waiting on the day
When the King's vengeance will come

Forgive me Jesus
Help me to forgive
Forgive me Jesus
Help me to forgive me
Jesus help me

Mercy is a river
Sometimes it washes clean
Sometimes it takes us to the brink
And back again

And the King's mercy will come
And the King's justice will come
It's not mine to repay
So soon will come the day
When the King's vengeance will come

All you wanted was a home cooked meal
I made you swallow such a bitter pill

LADDER

I found the ladder
But I could not climb
Stairwell of the stars
Leading up to heaven

I found the ladder
Want it to be mine
Foot by foot I fall down
Would I never be the one

To climb into space
To rise above it all
To look into God's own face
To see beyond it all

I found the ladder
But I could not climb
I had been hopeful
Of climbing up to heaven

Found that lonely ladder
Want it to be mine
I always seem to fall down
How I want to be the one

To climb into space
To rise above it all
To look into God's own face
To see beyond it all

Jesus pick me up
Carry me on up

LONGING

Long distance
The farthest shore
Separated by the years
But not for evermore
A sighing time
A pond of fear
A hoping tide
A path to clear

Sometimes it seems
Like a long day's journey
Into night school
Sometimes

Long distance
Another time and place
Another country dreams
Upon my face
Some long time soon
All will be clear
It won't seem long
At all
From there

Sometimes it seems
Like a long day's journey
Into night school
Sometimes

MAP

Line upon a page upon a map upon a
lap inside a cage of steel and rubber in
transit, glasses on the nose before the eyes
between the face and map's own page
what does it say? consult the signs,
landmarks, pedestrians, confusioning tales
of twists and turns right here and there
then round then right or left or on and stop
a light aglow arrive.

MODERN WORLD

This is the modern world
Plastic boys and plastic girls
Plastic toys are in a whirl

Use me and throw away
A new user, another day
I'm disposable anyway

Plastic faces, plastic hearts
Plastic people tear the world apart
In a modern world

Telephone across the globe
Can't talk to the one at home
In a crowd but you're on your own

Did they tell you life's like that
What did you want, a welcome mat?
A world of users will rob you bind
Just use you up and leave you crying

This is the modern world
Plastic boys and plastic girls
Broken toys are in a whirl

What we need – a tidal wave
To do our dishes day by day
And wash this little old world away

Plastic faces, plastic hearts
Plastic people tear the world apart
Modern world

in a little house there lived

MORE SECONDS

Second words not much to say
We eat our lunch then walk away
Stop talking, start talking
It's been so long 'till back in town
Did not know I would not be around
Stop talking, start talking
Put the blinkers on my eyes so I can clearly see
But sometimes I look inside not what's in front of me
Seconds ticking tilting over second best no not today that isn't you at all
Had to think it over
Does it mean less because it's real than simply chemical?
Fit my wheels down to the track so far ago
Don't know if I can roam the earth
Unbuckle my round shoes
So much to gain and lose but lost some anyway
Just one look can make you ask so many questions
So many questions
Can I afford to look again? Or not?

A NEW TOWN

Another time and place so far from where I live
Calls to me across the miles and years
Another attitude from what I've had to give
Transplants a heart of love over my fears

And though it seems so far away
I will be there some day

I'll be moving down to a new town
Moving down to a new town

Another way to live
Another frame of mind
Removes the doubt I held so hard so long
It's such a different world
Than what I leave behind
It's all I ever longed for all along

And though it seems so far away
I will be there some day

I'll be moving down to a new town
Moving down to a new town

I'll see my Jesus face to face
And revel in amazing grace
Then these shaded eyes will see
The wonders of his mercy

Moving down to a new town
Moving down to a new town

NEVER

I touched your arm
You grabbed my wrists
Never did receive
Never did receive your

Looked into your eyes
Into your eyes so full of mist
Never did receive
Never did receive your

Went our different ways
You sent me books drawn from your reading list
Gave me your interest and affection
Never did receive
Never did receive your love

NICE TALK (CONVERSATION FOR BEGINNERS)

Violently
We sit
And discuss the weather
What a nice day
While we put on our soft gloves
And inflict soft handed danger

So violently
Tiny dynamite
So softly, gently
Violently

Using consonants like clubs
Vowels like ropes
Nouns like steely blades
Verbs pound like fists raging
So sorry to beat and hurt you
With my innocent and carefree words

Violently
We sit, discussing weather
Nice day
We put our soft gloves on
Soft handed danger
We inflict so softly
Violently

NOBODY KNOWS

Nobody knows the trouble I've been to you
Except for you
And nobody knows the troubles you've seen me through
Except for you

And I'm sorry for the worry
I have put into your heart
I'm so sorry for the circumstance
That tears us both apart

Here I am now in a whirl
You're just an ordinary girl
And if I could
You know I would not doubt you
Here I am and there you are
It used to seem so very far
But now I know
I could not live without you

Nobody knows the trouble we've both been through
Except for you
And nobody knows the patience you've needed too
Except for you
I can't repay the kindness
I have taken from your hand
I can't begin to work it out
Or begin to understand

In a mixed up shook up world
You're just an ordinary girl
And if I could
You know I would not doubt you
Here I am and there you are
It used to seem so very far
But now I know
I could not live without you
Now I know
I could not live without you

OLD FRIENDS

Oh how the years go by, eh comrades?
Seems like such a little while
Since we said goodbye
Who said "life is a casting off"?
I would not shut you off
Perhaps I closed my eyes
and it all just slipped away

Old friends are never all that far away
Old friends never let each other down
Old friends are never all that far away
Old friends never let each other down

Oh how the years go by, eh comrades?
Pushing pencils all those years
The same clothes every day
Like the rain we fell to earth
And we hit the ground so hard
Ah, who could have known
it would be so many years?

Old friends are never all that far away
But old friends are sometimes far away
Old friends never let each other down
When you need them
Seems they've moved right out of town
So how come you bastards never came around?

Oh how the years go by
Eh comrades?
Life is no rehearsal after all
Doesn't mean we get things right first try

Perhaps I tried to call
But old memories got in the way
Now, perhaps, old hurts like all those years
Just fell away

Old friends are never all that far away
But old friends are often far away
Old friends never let each other down
But old friends can let each other down
Old friends are never all that far away
Sometimes old friends get tired of saying
hello in the street
Old friends never let each other down
Sometimes old friends don't follow through
with someone they'd like to see
Old friends are never all that far away
Sometimes old friends forget
what other people mean
But still, this does not mean
That we are not old friends

OVER

Enough sighing
Enough of wistful moments
I put my shoes on, I put my coat on

I'm passing it over, want to pass it over

Is anybody listening?
Does anybody hear?
Is it coming into focus?
Is the moment drawing near?
Doesn't matter if the invitations
Fall upon deaf eyes and ears
Compel anyone in earshot
Within arms reach
Within spitting distance

Is it over? I'm passing it over
Want to pass it over

Enough daydreams
Enough ought to be's
Time for talking less
Time for doing something

Is anybody listening?
Does anybody hear?
Is anybody listening?
Does anybody hear?
Are you listening?
Are you?
Are you?
Here?

PICTURES

Wednesday movie just begun
Seen it all before, another rerun
And there's a past in silver pictures on the wall
But you never saw no golden years
At all

Emotion
In pictures
Emotion

Scenes inside your lonely dreams
Your life a tragedy upon the screen
Focus softened by the years out of control
A fear of loss, you lost hold
Years ago

Emotion
In pictures
Emotion

Why is life so sad?
I don't know
Complex creature
B-grade feature
I don't know

 Looking for, look, looking for
Home movies of another life
This feature ends
New program starts
Tonight

PRODIGALUS
(DON'T THINK YOU CAN'T COME BACK)

Prodigal son is on the nose
Needs someone to wash his clothes
Wanted time to rant and roam
Now slap his face and send him home

RAIN

If I could find it in myself
To express some anger
at what you did
Maybe I would feel
like it's more commotion
Than you've deserved
Seeing all you left unsaid

So here's a little squall for you
A little thundercloud
A little rain
And if it darkens down your day
Perhaps your garden grows
Because of this

RECOVER ME

If I had a notion
To go drifting on the ocean
Could I count on you
To come and recover me

If I had a feeling
That my senses would go reeling
Could I take for true
That you would recover me

Come on, come on
Come on and recover me
Come on along, come on
Come on and recover me

Do I take it all for granted
There's so much I cannot see
Still I count on you
To come and recover me

Would not presume upon your mercy
But for all you've promised me
I know it's only you
Could come and recover me

Come on, come on
Come on and recover me
Such a singular emotion
To be lost out on the ocean
Oh, come on along, come on
And recover me

RIGHT ON TIME

One day when you're in desperate, desperate trouble
I'll come and get you out
Right on time, oh yes I will
Just you wait and see

And if you find yourself
Losing the struggle
Caving in
I will turn up to keep the roof from collapsing
Keep the struggle trolls from biting
Stop the plaster and tiles from hurting your sweet head
I'll be there then
On time, on time
Yes, oh yes I will
Just you wait and see

And if the tides are turning out against you
If the oceans seem too deep
I will beat against those waves
I will swim those endless seas
If it drags you down I will find you in those bitter depths
I will carry you to safe harbour
Right on time I will be there then
On time
On time, oh yes I will
Just you wait and see
Right on time I will be there then
On time, on time
Yes, oh yes I will
Just you wait and see
Just you wait and see

SAFE

Such secrets for a heart to carry
Such secrets

Come whisper all your stories
Of longing and loss
Come open up your buried treasure
Look at forgotten dreams together

You will be
Such secrets for a heart to carry
Safe with me
Such secrets

Come whisper all your stories
Of longing and loss
Like quiet prayers and lullabies
So soft the tears fall from your eyes

You will be
Such secrets for a heart to carry
Safe with me
Such secrets
You will be
Safe with me

Your secrets are safe with me
How can you bear a burden like this?
My yoke is easy, my burdens light
Come give them here, I'll give you rest

SELDOM RANDOM

Your thoughts, seldom random
Are higher than mine
Think some into my mind
See me some sights
Hear some hearings
Feel some feelings
Tasteful, touching
Breathe some air
So sensible I can almost taste it
Are you really in the details?

SEVENTY SEVEN SECONDS

Faith so blind

Faith so leaping

Don't run

Behind me

When I'm sleeping

Find a moment

Wait six seconds

I'll rewind

We'll see what beckons

Further thoughting

Fever thinking

Seven secondary ships

Are sinking

Eighteen candles (sic)

Windful wavers

Air and firing

Earthly favours

Sight is not

The time for walking

Sight is not

The time for walking

I think I might sit down now

SHAKE DOWN

Did you hear me?
Lost and lonely night time
My heart so full of raindrops
Did you hear?
I was waiting
I was listening for moonbeams
Did you hear me listening there?
So careful
So careful to put one foot
One careful foot
So carefully in front of
In front of another
Am I going not too slow?
Am I not rushing the moment?
Trying not to, not to, not...
Not to fall from a fever dream tightrope
Tight across my chest
Tight across my heart
One foot
Another ...with ...purpose?
Oh with careful fast not slow not purpose yes yet
Who can say
If you can hear me
Did you?

...and happily ever after

SMITH

Tone smithing
Bash caress stone and steel
Pluck a wavelength until you feel
Parenthesis and metaphor
Berate a word undue ensure

SOUTH

I am swimming, swimming
Caressing vast and endless oceans
Across these fluid fields of motion
Swimming free
So free

I am moving swimming free
Seeking stillness from the deeping
White as breaking, green as sleeping
Looking
Swimful free
So free

And I would cross the universe
If I thought I could
And saw the need
Across the fields of dreaming
To be close, so close
But I'm locked and keyed up here beneath
The south side of the sky
The south side of the sky

I am walking, walking
Possessed of handles, shoulders, notions
Such strange dreams of rolling oceans
Shadows, windows, desires, devotions
Clear my mind, unsettle side
Swim free
Swim free

SPEAK LOUDER

What you do speaks louder
Than the things you say
Your attitude informs each moment
Of the games you play
Behind the warmer smile
The inner core decays
Dark glasses shade the window of your soul
Actions speak louder than rock and roll

If ever doubts abounded let them come what may
Who you are is more
Than simply what you say
But it's nice to hear it
Spoken rightly anyway
Tell me, is your heart out of control?
Actions speak louder than rock and roll

No need to sing and dance
About the life you lead
A modest heart will soon
Be lifted up indeed
But if you doubt the wisdom
Of the word and deed
Empty talk won't satisfy the soul
Actions speak louder than rock and roll

STAND YOUR GROUND

Trapped by both sides
Numbed by mediocrity
Lashed by hypocrisy
Taunted by cultural baggage
Tied to your back
Laughed at severely by the desire to possess
Soul torn to shreds by the claws of loneliness
Candy stolen from you baby by the lure of false glamour
Diseased and disposed of by vanity's hammer

Stand your ground
Stand for something
Don't get thrown around
Stand your ground

TENDER HUMAN HEART

Did they hurt you
My tender hearted human
Did they hurt you
Did they take your fragile soul
And break it up into
A million tiny pieces

Did they hurt you
My fragile, fragile human
Did they hurt you
Did they strip you of your jewels
Trample precious pearls
Into the muddy ground

It would need a touch
So much more gentle than mine
To ease away your pain
It would need the love
Of a heavenly father's hand
To heal your hurt
And make you whole again

Did they hurt you
My tender hearted human
Did they hurt you
Did they trample on your innocence
And leave your broken heart
Without defence

It would need a touch
So much more gentle than mine
To ease away your pain
It would need the love
Of a heavenly father's hand
To heal your hurt
And make you whole again

TIDE

I stood upon the shore
Looked into the lapping waves
I wondered if I'd see you there

Wondered if I could commit myself
To the cold green ocean
Bring about your rescue
Without going under too

Lost at sea
All I can offer you is words
And hope you wrap the truth
Like oxygen
Around your air starved lungs

TOLD

I told you
At least I thought I did
I never meant the things I said
To sound like something unconsidered
I told you
Once or twice - or so I think
I never would have hurt you
If you listened to my heart
And not the words I never said
Ah, in the telling lies a tale
A tale telling lies inside
Don't you listen
Don't you hear
You know me
Is my hope never clear?
Five farthings
Tolled the bell

WALK AWAY FROM THE FIRE

I was trying to stay warm beside the crimson glow
Such a chill in the air, warm the firelight drew me close
It seemed like every passer by knew me by name
They asked me if I knew the one to blame

(A fire in the hearth)
They asked me who I knew
I said I don't know
Some barnyard animal called me a liar
I wished that I had walked away
From the fire

He'd warned me that evening that I would deny
I told Him I could not conceive such a lie
I'd always thought that I would die for His name
But now it seems like everything has changed

(A fire in the heart)
They asked me who I knew
I said I don't know
Some barnyard animal called me a liar
I wished that I had walked away
From the fire

In the heat of the moment I turned away
I clung for life to a warmth that passed away
In the heat of the moment
I let him down
And the siren of the morning
Sends chills down my spine

I wish I had walked away from the fire
I wish I had walked away from the fire

Burned by both sides

WALK IN THE WATER

Water
Cool water
Down by the river
I walk in the water

I walked into the water
Cold and deep
I lay down in the water
Experienced a mystery

Water and earth come bury me
Bury the dark once alive in me
God come and breathe life into me
Lift me up

Lead me down into the water
Cold and deep
Lay me down in the water
Let me see a mystery

Water and earth come bury me
Bury the dark once alive in me
God come and breathe life into me
Lift me up

WHAT

All you want
All you ever really want
Is a taste
Of what you need
All you want
Is a little attention
Mercy baby mercy what you need

I know I talk too much
All I got is a life beat up
Wring out my emotions
Every drop of sweat and blood
Can't change the fact you need a change
In your lifetime
Mercy cry for mercy
What you need

All you want
All you ever really want
Is a taste
Of sweet eternity
All you want
Is a little attention
Mercy baby mercy what you need

WHERE

Ask me to wait and I will to turn and you are gone
Now this I did not know where did you go?
Tell me things I'm thinking I will tell you ask me not
and I will head right home where did you go I do not know
Look right back as I see you, swim into your eyes
like liquid I could drown inside I turned around
and you are gone, where did you go, where did you go?

Don't think you have a thing to prove
Don't think you have a debt to owe
I just wonder if you're keeping close to well
Don't think you have a tale to tell
That will not wait for ears to hear
Your perfect, shudder diminishing aficionado is still here
As always here
But where are you?
Where did you go?

Ask me not to wait up and maybe I just can't help
It's not a night for sleeping anyway
Parallel to morning dawning, dusk disintegrating
Borrow no fear like love's long cast away imperfection
Just be calm, becalm your unexpectable, unavoidable insurrection
What could be so necessary
So plain
So clear
So how or why or where
Why aren't you here?

WHY CAN'T I HOLD YOU?

Across the fields and plains
Across the tides and flames
Beyond the floods and rains
Lie promises and dreams
Before the trees and earth
Beneath the stars and moon
Below the clouds and birds
Lie words and hopes and schemes

Why can't you speak to this
Why can't you hear my heart
Why can't you see your part
Why can't I hold you?
Why can't I find the word
Why can't I hear it spoken
Why must my heart be broken
Why can't I hold you

WINE AND WATER

They're turning wine back into water
Taking mud out of your eye
Restoring illness to the daughter
Taking sight back from the blind
Lay down Lazarus you can't do that
Stop weeping Jesus, don't know what came over that dead man
They're turning wine
Back into water
Once again

WORDSTUFF

So I see you've heard some words
Until you earn them though, lifeless they remain
You can't steal them from another
Or borrow from a kindly friend

WORTH

Doesn't take much
To cause a little ruckus
Takes almost nothing at all
To shake a rattle at it all
Takes more than just a little
To be somewhat inhospitable
For what it's worth, come on
Come down to earth

It takes nothing to be kind
Sometimes things need a rewind
If polite is not in sight
No wonder it's goodnight
Too less than easy going much of the time

Doesn't take much
To take a breath before digestion
Responding less in kind
An easy going mind makes everything
Less than full of stressing

Takes nothing, nothing to be kind
Much less than impolite
Good morning is in sight
Easy going more of the time

Takes nothing, nothing to be kinder
Than the way it just began
Breathe deep, deep and easy
Nothing
Nothing needed beyond a smile
Saturate a little while
And take it easy

WRITE

Spidered, spidery
threads of
ink and feeling
deprive the page of
purity, stealing back
its blank potential and
instead rendering it
potent, the pollutives
bringing closer a
true ecology necessary,
needful, desirable.
What are words *for*
if not to slap on
virgin paper?

YOU WILL GO FREE

Some things are not written in wet concrete
Some things are not hidden with invisible ink
Some things are not put down on paper you can tear up
You didn't even sign the contract
You didn't even slit your wrists
To seal the covenant
All you ask for was agreed
Some day
You will go free

Not talking about the bonds that give you no direction
Not talking about the anchor leaves you drifting
Not talking about a freedom of choice that is no choice but what you're told you know you want
A thousand million Coke and Nintendo rebels against the perceived
And not the real
You're not like that (much)
Not that you have much say in it
You didn't even sign the contract
You didn't even slit your wrists
To seal the covenant
All you were asked was to agree
Some day
Some day you will go free

If it was a question you could answer
Would you like to be wet jelly without a bowl
A frame without an image
A shoe without a sole
A word without a meaning
A watch without a battery
A battery without a torch or toy
A shirt without a skin to be covering
You didn't even sign the contract
You didn't even slit your wrists
To seal the covenant
All you were asked was to agree
Some day
Some day you will go free

You are without boundaries
You are without skin to hold you in
Free
So free (that's what you told me)
Who can separate you from your own skin
Do or don't believe it's true
It's true
You will
Go

THANKS

Thank you for reading, first of all.

This time around I have taken the opportunity to regather so much of my early work, so much out of print. This edition of To Cut a Long Story Short borrows its title and almost all of the contents from my second self-published collection from 1998, as well as works from the earlier homemade chapbook Moment to Moment. I have also included song lyrics from my days writing for the band Perfect Stranger, plus a stray, occasional previously unseen piece.

The tricky part of revisiting things you created years ago is the temptation to edit and/or rewrite; I confess to tidying up the odd phrase or word here and there but have tried not to tamper with what younger me was saying.

Once again, some of the words in this collection are me
some is friends and friends of friends
some is speculation, pure and simple
and some of it is simply enjoying the gravity, sound and sauce of simple words placed alongside each other.

If you are someone I know or have known, or not, I hope you find something of yourself in these pages.

And again, I hope you have fun with what you read.

Many thanks for encouragement, critique, inspiration and friendship on the journey; Adam, Andy & Kathy, Angela, Brian, Craig, Graham, Howie and Beth, Jared, Jono and Al, Justin, Kate, Kevin and Jan, Kingsley, Kristel and New Song Fridays, Leo, Matt & Kareen, Mike and Jane, PT, Pieter, Steve, Stu, Vic, Wes and all the you-know-who-you-are people I haven't named, whether for modesty or amnesia.

Many thanks to my family.

ABOUT THE AUTHOR

Martin Fawkes' love of word play began at an early age.

"I remember writing poems in primary school, and the teacher calling my parents in to chat about them, like I'd done something really good, which I never quite believed".

Over time, however, it dawned on him this word play might be worth pursuing. Subsequent years in rock bands meant lots of songwriting, honing his poetry and storytelling skills into musical form.

Spoken word gigs followed, as did chapbooks and self-published collections of poetry and lyrics.

Now, many years later, here we are, a properly published poet. You hold in your hands one of a four part sequence, celebrating a lifetime of writing.

- **Worlds We Leave Behind** (works 2010-2023)
- **Love, Devotion, Surrender and other bright ideas** (works mainly from early 2000's)
- **To Cut a Long Story Short** (earlier works)
- **Surprise Visitors and other stories:** Christmas poems

www.ingramcontent.com/pod-product-compliance
Lightning Source LLC
Chambersburg PA
CBHW072016290426
44109CB00018B/2261